Mixing it up with . . .

Football

Also available in the same series:

Owen Smith, *Mixing it up with . . . The Simpsons*
Owen Smith, *Mixing it up with . . . Harry Potter*

Mixing it up with . . .

Football

10 sessions about faith for 9–13s

Owen Smith

CHURCH HOUSE PUBLISHING

Church House Publishing
Church House
Great Smith Street
London SW1P 3AZ
Tel: 020 7898 1451
Fax: 020 7898 1449

ISBN 978-0-7151-4105-2

Published 2007 by Church House Publishing.

Cover design by www.penquinboy.net
Printed in England by Halstan and Co. Ltd, Amersham, Bucks

contents

Introduction

How this book came about

Six months after I started work at St Margaret's Church, Rainham, Kent, I carried out a review of all our activities with young people to identify which groups we were working with and which we were failing to reach. As part of that review, it became clear that there were certain gaps in our work. One such gap was suitable provision for the ten- and eleven-year-old boys, who were too young to come along to the church youth group and either found that the style of the Sunday morning provision we had at the time didn't cater to their interests, or were unable to come at all on Sunday because of football matches and other commitments.

We identified some boys who came from families within the congregation and some who were known to us through outreach projects we had recently run in the local community, and invited them to a midweek group, later dubbed 'Superb'. As I looked round for material aimed at the nine to thirteen age group, I found that there was very little available and even less that capitalized on the interests of young people of this age.

With this in mind, I set about writing some material that used examples of the culture in which these young people were immersed to introduce and explore relevant Christian themes. These sessions are the result!

Who is this material for?

A recent study found that more young people stopped coming to church at the age of eleven than at any other age.[1] Yet this is an age group that is largely under-resourced by churches. This material is suitable for young people aged nine to thirteen who already have some church involvement and also for those on the fringe who may find it too difficult to come to other church activities for cultural reasons or because the times of regular church groups are inconvenient.

As the activities do not require a huge amount of space, the material may be used with a midweek group, a Sunday school, or a school lunchtime group. Each session lasts about 45 minutes, but the length can be tailored to suit your individual setting. Forty-five minutes is only long enough to provide an introduction to a topic. If in the course of the sessions you find that a certain issue or question is of particular interest to your young people, you can go back to it and cover it in greater depth at a later date.

Working with nine- to thirteen-year-olds

Young people between nine and thirteen are undergoing a huge number of changes – both physically and mentally. They are about to embark on the often treacherous journey through adolescence and are beginning to know their own mind. They are moving away from their parents towards their peers and are developing the sense of self that they'll carry with them into their adult lives.[2] They have a new-found capacity for abstract thought and can now consider a variety of opinions and possible outcomes, thinking through situations without needing concrete experiences.[3] All this means that groups and activities for this age range should differ from those aimed at younger children or teenagers.

Setting up a group

When setting up a group, there are a number of things it's important to consider.

Who is your group aimed at?

First, you need to decide:

- Is it a group that provides an opportunity for young people with no previous contact with the church to start to think about some Christian themes?

- Is it a group that seeks to nurture and encourage the young people who are already part of the church community?

- Is it a combination of the two?

You might also want to think about whether your young people will feel more comfortable meeting in a single-sex group. This will depend on the personalities and the gender breakdown of the young people you are aiming at.

When to hold your group

You need to identify the best time for your group to meet. It might be that you will use this material with a group as part of your provision for children and young people on a Sunday morning. You might find, however, as we did, that Sunday is not a good time for nine- to thirteen-year-olds to come to a group such as this. Many play sports and have other activities and commitments on Sunday mornings. Thankfully, we are moving away from the idea that church and worship only take place on a Sunday, and it may be that your work with this age group needs a 'fresh expression' of church. For more about such groups and initiatives, have a look at the fresh expressions web site – www.freshexpressions.org.uk.

Venue

It's also important to have thought through the 'where' of your group. The venue for your sessions is very important in determining how your group will run – the environment can have a huge impact on how a session goes. It may be that you have limited options over where you can meet. But you do need a room free of major distractions and big enough to allow your group to relax in comfort. You will also need a television and a DVD player. Possible venues might include the home of a member of the group, the vicarage (as long as you've asked the vicar first!)or the church hall. Wherever you decide to meet, you must make sure that you are following the child protection guidelines set by your Church or organization – more about this below.

Ground rules

As your group begins to meet, you may find it useful to come up with some kind of agreement about how the group will work. Obviously you don't want the sessions to feel like school, but it's often good to get your young people to come up with a few basic ground rules that set out what is expected of each member, including you, and what behaviour is not acceptable to the group. These rules might include the group's thoughts about how they should treat one another and treat the place in which you meet. Some rules could also be included to make sure that your group is a 'safe' environment where everyone feels able to contribute to the discussions. Such rules might include keeping within the group the things different people share during sessions, rather than talking about them to other friends afterwards, and making sure that everyone gets a chance to say what they think without being interrupted.

Group identity

Establishing a strong group identity and a sense of ownership of the group is essential when working with nines to thirteens. These young people are at a point in their lives when 'belonging' is very important. While being careful not to set up cliques, you need to make your group one to which the young people feel attached. This can be an important part of maintaining their interest, particularly as they make the transition from primary to secondary education. When I started a group, I got the young people to come up with a name during the first session. Introducing regular occurrences unique to the group can also help to bond the young people. These might be simple things like always having doughnuts when it's someone's birthday, having some sort of reward if a group member brings their own Bible to a session or giving a prize to the first person to find the Bible passage.

Good practice: child protection and health and safety

It's important that you make yourself aware of the guidelines your organization has in place to protect you as a leader and the young people you are working with. These will probably take the form of a child protection policy and good practice guidelines, and will be available from your Diocesan, or your denomination's, Children's or Youth Officer. Making yourself aware of these guidelines is a key part of preparing yourself to run a group. On the basis of these guidelines, you will need to consider how many leaders your group will need to have present when it meets. For young people over eight, the normal ratio is one leader for every eight young people, with a minimum of two leaders. You will also need to consider what contact information and parental permission you need to seek from the young people who will attend your group.

For more information on matters relating to child protection and best practice, get in touch with your Diocesan Youth Officer, or your denomination's equivalent, who will be happy to give you further advice.

Handling sensitive issues

Some of the sessions in this book cover topics that might bring up issues that will be sensitive for particular members of the group. Talking about subjects such as families, or self-image, might raise both positive and negative anxieties, memories and experiences. If a young person shares such feelings, it may be appropriate to talk them through as part of the discussion during the session – young people are often surprisingly mature when it appears that a member of their group is hurting. Sometimes, however, it might be better to suggest gently that you talk to the young person at a more suitable time. Be careful, though, not to diminish the importance of what they have said or want to share. If at any point you feel that you are getting out of your depth – don't keep going! It may be that you need to talk to your vicar or line-manager about getting help from someone with more experience in dealing with such issues. You don't have to know all the answers, but knowing where to find out more is a good start!

Encouraging your group to talk

Some of the activities included within the sessions involve discussion, and this might prove difficult for some groups. Some young people will feed off one another's ideas and will be able to hold interesting and lively discussions. In such groups, make sure that one or two people aren't monopolizing the discussion. You might need to draw in the quieter members of the group, gently inviting them to contribute, remembering that they might not want to say anything! If the discussion becomes too rowdy, you might need to pause for a moment and make sure that members take turns to contribute their opinions.

When faced with a question for discussion, other groups will sit in silence, avoiding eye contact with anyone in the room. Initially, don't worry about silence – it might just take a moment for the young people to process what you are asking. However, if the silence persists, you may need to restate the question, breaking it down into simpler ideas. Use open questions to stimulate the discussion – questions that can't simply be answered by a 'yes' or a 'no'. Sometimes, it may work better to ask the group to discuss a particular issue from the point of view of a third party within a scenario. Some groups will find it much easier to talk about how 'David' or 'Helen' might feel or act in a certain situation, rather than how they themselves would feel or act.

Why use contemporary culture?

Using the culture of the day to help engage people in thinking about Christian themes is not a new idea! When Jesus taught the people he met on his travels, he used stories and illustrations firmly rooted in the culture of the time. The parables he used to convey his messages had agricultural or social settings with which his audience would have been able to identify.

In the past, the Church has sometimes appeared more wary of the ever-expanding influence that media such as television and film have on people, sometimes perceiving them more as a threat than an aid. Today, young people coming to the end of primary school and starting secondary education are immersed in a culture of satellite TV, Playstations, celebrities, *Big Brother* and footballers. It is a culture where 'anything goes' and 'want it *now*' seem to be the prevailing philosophies. In order to engage with these young people we need to use the heroes and images they encounter daily to explore what are often, to them, unfamiliar Christian themes.

Many aspects of contemporary culture can be used to introduce and explore Christian themes. If the interests of the young people in your group lie more in music than football, then lyrics from their favourite songs might be an excellent basis for a session. You might want to look at resources such as *Music to Move the Soul*[4] for examples of such material. *Youthwork Magazine* www.youthwork.co.uk has regular features showing how different aspects of youth culture can be used in this way.

The Internet is an amazing tool for developing such sessions – you can find episode summaries, plot synopses, quotations from films and lyrics for songs, as well as a wealth of background material and trivia.

Why use football?

In 2002, a survey of young people aged eight to fifteen found that 57 per cent of boys and 18 per cent of girls regularly played football outside school hours, playing, on average, 27 minutes each day.[5] Much of the time and money of many nine- to thirteen-year-old boys are taken up with playing football, watching football and keeping up with the current kit, line-up and successes of their favourite football team. With this in mind, having decided to write material for this age group, I felt that using football as a means of introducing and exploring Christian themes was a logical next step.

A particular challenge posed by using football as a theme was that those young people who play football tend to be more physical – they like to get up and do things rather than listen or read. Each session therefore needed to involve a balance of activity and inactivity, coupled with a consideration of the space likely to be available. As you read through these suggestions, you may, of course, need to adapt them for your own group.

Caution!

It might be said that some aspects of football display attitudes and behaviour that we would not want to encourage in our young people. There will, however, always be elements of popular culture that are not, as Paul said, as good, as pure or as admirable as we would like (Philippians 4.8). It is our responsibility to make it clear to our young people that there are features of the culture in which we live that are good and to be encouraged, and features that we need to be more wary of. As Christians we cannot establish ourselves as islands detached from the culture that permeates all areas of our lives – Jesus called us to be in the world, but not of it. We need to support our young people as they form their opinions of the world around them, and equip them with the ability to discern those things that are not acceptable.

The shape of this book

This book contains ten sessions, each of which deals with a basic idea central to Christian faith. Each session lasts about 45 minutes. The material aims not only to get young people to engage with a range of themes, but also to get them reading the Bible and praying together as a group.

The shape of each session

Beforehand . . . This tells the person leading the group about any preparation that will need to be done before the session.

Opening activity . . . This activity introduces the session's theme and its purpose is to get the young people thinking about the issue. It is usually quite short, lasting between 5 and 15 minutes.

Football focus . . . The theme for the session is explored further, and is related to the particular aspect of football being considered in that session. There are questions for discussion either as a whole group, or in smaller groups, pairs or threes who then feed back their ideas to the whole group.

Bible focus . . . The young people look up a Bible verse that deals with the Christian perspective on the session's theme. Here the verses are quoted from the NIV, but you might like to use the version your group members know best.

Prayer response . . . Each session ends with a prayer activity drawing on the session's theme and giving the young people a chance to respond in some way.

Some sessions feature an activity or further information: this is included as a photocopiable sheet at the end of the session.

Thanks

The writing of this book has involved the patience of a lot of people, to all of whom I owe a great deal! I'd like to thank my Superb cell group (Ross, Alex, Tom, Jack, Joe, Connor, Craig, John, David, Fenner and Nick), for helping me refine the sessions and telling me what they thought with no holds barred! I'd like to thank the youth groups and youth workers of St Mary's Church, Tonbridge, the parish of Rochester and Christchurch, Chislehurst, for trying out the sessions and sending me their feedback. Finally, my thanks go to my boss Canon Alan Vousden for enduring my constant mess in his nice clean office, and to our wonderful Rochester Diocesan Youth Advisor Phil Greig for making me think about publishing these sessions in the first place.

Notes

[1] Peter Brierley, *Reaching and Keeping Tweenagers*, Christian Research Association, 2003.
[2] Erik H. Erikson, *Identity: Youth and Crisis*, W. W. Norton, 1968.
[3] Jean Piaget (translated by W. Mays), *The Principles of Genetic Epistemology*, Routledge, 1972.
[4] Steve and Ruth Adams, *Music to Move the Soul*, Spring Harvest, 2003.
[5] UK 2000 Time Use Survey: www.statistics.gov.uk/timeuse/default.asp.

fans
GOD'S GREAT LOVE FOR US

SESSION AIM . . . . . . **To understand that God knows everything about us and loves us just as we are**

FOOTBALL FOCUS . . . Football fans

BIBLE FOCUS . . . . . . 'O LORD, you have searched me and you know me.
You know when I sit and when I rise;
   you perceive my thoughts from afar.
You discern my going out and my lying down;
   you are familiar with all my ways.
Before a word is on my tongue you know it completely, O LORD.
You hem me in – behind and before;
   you have laid your hand upon me.
Such knowledge is too wonderful for me,
   too lofty for me to attain.
Where can I go from your Spirit?
   Where can I flee from your presence?
If I go up to the heavens, you are there;
   if I make my bed in the depths, you are there.
If I rise on the wings of the dawn, if I settle on the far side of the sea,
   even there your hand will guide me, your right hand will hold me fast.
If I say, "Surely the darkness will hide me and the light become night around me,"
   even the darkness will not be dark to you;
the night will shine like the day, for darkness is as light to you.
For you created my inmost being;
   you knit me together in my mother's womb.
I praise you because I am fearfully and wonderfully made;
   your works are wonderful, I know that full well.
My frame was not hidden from you when I was made in the secret place.
When I was woven together in the depths of the earth, your eyes saw my unformed body.
All the days ordained for me were written in your book before one of them came to be.'

(Psalm 139.1-16)

RESOURCES . . . . *Large sheets of paper, pens, Bible, background music, copies of Resource sheet 1*

●   Photocopy enough copies of Resource sheet 1 to give one copy to each group of young people.

A true fan

(5 minutes)

Begin the session by asking who would say they are true football fans – have a show of hands. Choose a few of those who have put up their hands and ask them if they would like to take the 'True Football Fans Test' – the test that proves that a person is 100 per cent football crazy.

Ask the following questions:

1 What year did England last win the World Cup? (1966)
2 How many clubs are there in the Premiership? (20)
3 What is the highest number of goals scored by one team in a single Premiership game? (9)
4 What is the minimum length of a football pitch? (90 m)
5 How many pentagons make up the traditional black and white football? (32)
6 What can a goalkeeper be booked for, that no other player can be booked for? (Rolling his sleeves up, as the ref must be able to distinguish who touches a ball within a group of players)
7 Which team's stadium was the first in Europe to have floodlights installed? (Sheffield United)
8 What was the football originally made out of? (A pig's bladder!)
9 How many matches were played in the 2006 World Cup? (64)
10 Think of the first player to get sent off during a Cup Final: which team did he play for? (Manchester United)

How did they do – are they true football fans?

Fan-Tastic

(15 minutes)

So what does it take to be a true football fan? If aliens came to earth, how could they spot the true football fans from the people who were just slightly interested? What would they look like? What characteristics would they have? What would they know? What equipment would they have? Divide the young people into small groups and give each group a copy of Resource sheet 1. Get them to draw and label a picture of a true football fan. Give the groups 5 minutes to come up with their drawings and then feed back their ideas to the whole group.

Number 1 fan

(10 minutes)

Each of us has a fan – someone who follows our every move from our beginning right through to our end and knows everything about us. Get the group to look up Psalm 139.

- Who does verse 1 say is our biggest fan? (God.)
- What does God know and do that shows us that he is our fan? (He knows everything about us, and goes with us wherever we go. God will never stop supporting us just because we don't do very well or because someone better than us comes along.)
- Why is God a fan of ours? (He created us and made us to be exactly as we are.)
- Who does this psalm apply to? (Everyone!)

Thanks!

(10 minutes)

God really is head over heels about us – he loves us more than we can possibly imagine. Part of our worship should be to thank him for this – we are often very good at asking God for what we want but we forget to say thank you.

Lay out some large pieces of paper in the middle of the group. Pass round the pens and play some music while giving the young people the opportunity to fill the paper with words and pictures of things for which they want to say thank you to God. Encourage them to do this without talking to one another – explain that this is an activity through which they can thank God for all the good gifts he's given us.

After a period of time, finish the activity by saying a short prayer thanking God for his goodness to us. Either choose your own prayer or use the one below.

Dear God,
Thank you that you are our number one fan.
Thank you that wherever we go, whatever we do,
    you are with us, guiding and supporting us.
Help us to remember to say thank you.
Amen.

I spy a football fan!
A SPOTTER'S GUIDE

In the box below draw and label your picture of a football fan.
How would our alien friends know what to look for if they landed on earth?

Picked for the team
GOD'S PRIORITIES

SESSION AIM....... **To understand that God does not judge us on our skills – he loves us whatever**

FOOTBALL FOCUS.... The Dream Team

BIBLE FOCUS....... 'But the LORD said to Samuel, "Do not consider his appearance or his height, for I have rejected him. The LORD does not look at the things man looks at. Man looks at the outward appearance, but the LORD looks at the heart." (1 Samuel 16.7)

RESOURCES......... *Paper, pens, jelly babies, Bible, copies of Resource sheet 2*

- Photocopy enough copies of Resource sheet 2 to give one copy to each small group.

The Dream Team
(10 minutes)
Begin the session by dividing the young people into pairs or small groups. Hand each group a copy of Resource sheet 2 and give them 5 minutes to come up with their Dream Team – the perfect football team. They can choose players past or present from any team and of any nationality. Who would they choose in order to have the best chance of winning the championship? Once groups have chosen their teams, get them to feed back to the whole group.

The criteria
(10 minutes)
How did they decide who to include in their dream team? As a group, come up with a brain-dump of all the different factors or characteristics that led them to choose one player over another. What aspects of a player did they think were important? They might include answers such as fitness, goals scored so far this season, number of captaincies, etc.

When the group have come up with as many ideas as they can think of, ask them to go back to their small groups and pick their top three criteria – the three most important things they would look for when choosing players to join their team.

FOCUS
on Bible passage

Little ol' David

(*10 minutes*)

Either read 1 Samuel 16.1-13, or tell the story of how Samuel came to choose David as the next king. Get the young people to think about the following questions:

- When Samuel explained to Jesse why he had come, who do you think Jesse expected Samuel to choose? (Eliab – his eldest son. In those days, the eldest son held a position of responsibility. Most privileges would have fallen to him.)
- How do you think the brothers felt when David was anointed king?
- Look at verse 7 in particular – why do you think God doesn't go by people's outward appearance when he judges them? (Because that's not the important part. How a person acts and thinks, and where their priorities lie, are what are important.)

PRAYER
response

Jelly babies!

(*10 minutes*)

Unfortunately, we're all guilty of judging other people without bothering to get to know them – we all make decisions about other people that might not necessarily be true. Some people feel they might never quite fit in because they're always thought of as being geeky or unfashionable or annoying. We need to pray for these people and the other people around us.

Encourage the group to think of someone they know who they might be guilty of judging unfairly or someone they know who is always left out because they don't seem to fit in. Go round the circle and get everyone to take a jelly baby and say a short prayer for their person. If possible, get them to say their prayer aloud. However, if your group is not comfortable with doing this, encourage them to pray silently, saying 'Amen' out loud to let the next person know it's their turn to pray. They can eat their jelly baby once they've said their prayer.

Finish the activity with a short prayer of your choosing or use the one below.

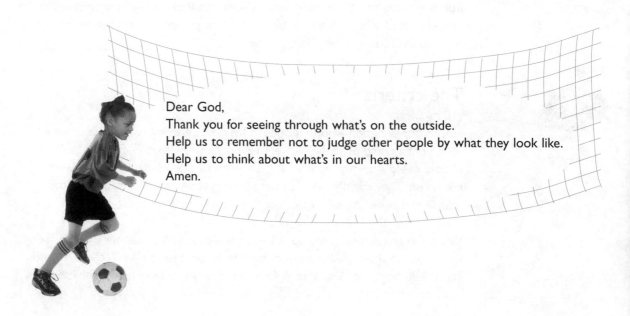

Dear God,
Thank you for seeing through what's on the outside.
Help us to remember not to judge other people by what they look like.
Help us to think about what's in our hearts.
Amen.

The Dream Team

Who would you choose to play in your perfect football team?
Write the names of the players, past or present, in the shirts to make up your dream team.

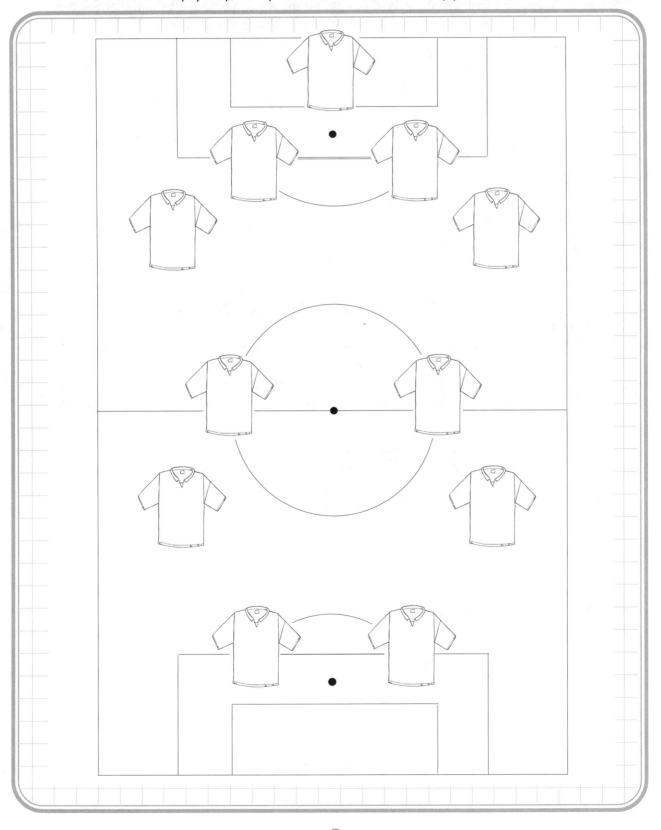

Goal!!!
SIN

SESSION AIM......... **To think about how our sin means we don't quite hit the target but that Jesus' death meant that we can be put right with God**

FOOTBALL FOCUS... Scoring goals

BIBLE FOCUS....... 'For all have sinned and fall short of the glory of God, and are justified freely by his grace through the redemption that came by Christ Jesus.' (Romans 3.23-24)

RESOURCES......... *Football and goals (or 'pin the football on the goal' game), Bible, paper, pens, bin, copies of Resource sheet 3*

BEFOREHAND

- If you have space, put up a set of football goals for the first activity. Or . . .
- Prepare the 'pin the football on the goal' activity.
- Photocopy enough copies of Resource sheet 3 to give one to each group.

OPENING activity

GOOOOOOOOOOOOOOOOOOOAL!
(10 minutes)

Get one of the group to be goalie, while the other young people take turns in trying to score a goal. Once everyone has had a go, give them another go, but this time blindfold them first. **Note:** When the young people are blindfolded, *they should not take a run-up*, but should shoot from a standing position. For health and safety reasons, make this clear to them before you start.

If you don't have enough space for the above activity, play a version of 'pin the tail on the donkey'. Put a piece of paper with a football goal on it on the wall. Blindfold players one at a time, spin them round, and then get them to stick a football as close to the middle of the goal as they can. *Take care to make sure the players are safe while blindfolded.*

Once everyone who wants to has had a chance to take part in the activity, introduce the theme of the session – scoring goals and missing the mark.

FOCUS on football

Missing the mark
(15 minutes)

Picture your life each day as a bit like trying to score a goal. We have a target (or goal) to aim at, and this is to try to live our lives in the way God wants us to. This means doing the things we know are good, and trying not to do the things we know are bad – which the Bible calls 'sin'.

As in football, sometimes we hit the target but at other times we miss – perhaps only just. But whether we hit the crossbar, or drive the ball well into the crowd, we've still missed the target.

Divide the young people into smaller groups and give each group a copy of Resource sheet 3. Get the young people to write down inside the goal reasons why a footballer might miss the mark and shoot wide. Then get them to come up with what might tempt *them* to do things they know aren't good and make them miss the standard God has set for us. Write these ideas down outside the goal.

Give the groups 5 minutes to come up with their ideas and then feed them back to the group.

FOCUS
on Bible passage

Missed!

(*10 minutes*)

Ask the group whether anyone has ever missed a shot while playing football? Who has never done something they know they shouldn't?

All of us miss the goal pretty much every day. None of us are perfect – we all do things that we know are wrong. Get the group to look up Romans 3.23.

● What does this verse say? (We've all failed to live up to God's standards.)

Once the group has understood the message of verse 23, get someone to read verse 24. The language in verse 24 is very 'churchy', so you might want to make sure that the group understand all the terms used. These are

● 'justified freely' – we are made right with God;
● 'by his grace' – by God's love in giving us so much more than we deserve;
● 'through the redemption that came by Christ Jesus' – because Jesus took the punishment for all the times we missed the goal.

Get the group to think about the following question:

● What promise does God make to us in this verse? (Because Jesus died on the cross to take the punishment for all the times we missed the target and did something wrong, we don't have to pay the price for our sins – our relationship with God is made perfect again.)

PRAYER
response

Bin it

(*10 minutes*)

Hand each member of the group a piece of paper and a pen. Get the young people to write down one or more things that they want to say sorry to God for. At what times and in what situations have they missed the goal? Emphasize that no one else will see what they write, so they can be honest. When everyone has finished, get them to screw up their pieces of paper and throw them into the bin as a sign that they are saying sorry to God for whatever they have written.

Finish the activity with a prayer, either one of your own or the one below, and make sure that the papers are disposed of afterwards so that no one reads what was written.

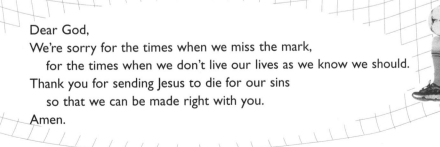

Dear God,
We're sorry for the times when we miss the mark,
    for the times when we don't live our lives as we know we should.
Thank you for sending Jesus to die for our sins
    so that we can be made right with you.
Amen.

Come up with reasons why a footballer might miss the mark and shoot wide, and write them inside the goal below. Outside the goal, write things that might tempt you to do things that you know aren't right.

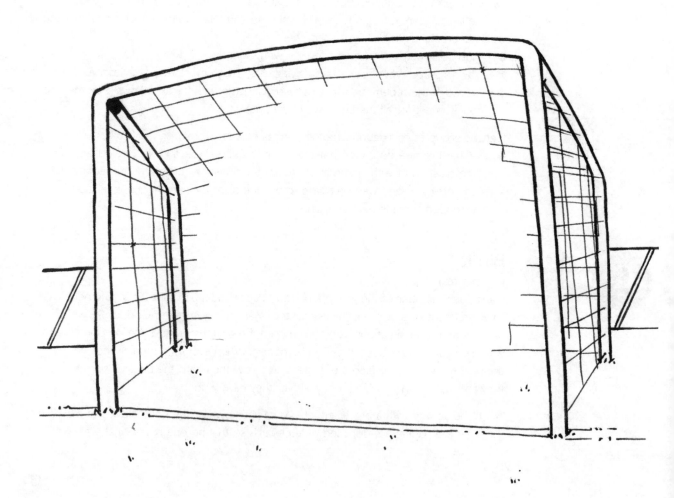

Rules and regulations
THE TEN COMMANDMENTS

SESSION AIM ...... **To think about the importance of having rules to guide us**

FOOTBALL FOCUS.... The rules of football

BIBLE FOCUS....... 'I am the LORD your God, who brought you out of Egypt,
out of the land of slavery.
You shall have no other gods before me.
You shall not make for yourself an idol in the form of anything in
heaven above or on the earth beneath or in the waters below.
You shall not bow down to them or worship them; for I, the LORD your
God, am a jealous God, punishing the children for the sin of the
fathers to the third and fourth generation of those who hate me, but
showing love to a thousand generations of those who love me and
keep my commandments.
You shall not misuse the name of the LORD your God, for the
LORD will not hold anyone guiltless who misuses his name.
Remember the Sabbath day by keeping it holy. Six days
you shall labour and do all your work, but the seventh day
is a Sabbath to the LORD your God. On it you shall not do
any work, neither you, nor your son or daughter, nor your
manservant or maidservant, nor your animals, nor the alien
within your gates. For in six days the LORD made the
heavens and the earth, the sea, and all that is in them, but he
rested on the seventh day. Therefore the LORD blessed the
Sabbath day and made it holy.
Honour your father and your mother, so that you may live long
in the land the LORD your God is giving you.
You shall not murder.
You shall not commit adultery.
You shall not steal.
You shall not give false testimony against your neighbour.
You shall not covet your neighbour's house. You shall not covet your neighbour's wife,
or his manservant or maidservant, his ox or donkey, or anything that belongs to
your neighbour.' (Exodus 20.2-17)

RESOURCES......... *Football, large sheet of paper, markers, pens, Bible, copies of Resource sheet 4*

- Make sure you are familiar with some of the rules of the game of football.
  Resource sheet 4a gives an overview of the basic rules.
- Photocopy on to card and then cut up enough copies of Resource sheet 4b
  to give each young person the outline of a stone tablet.

A game of several halves

(5 minutes)

Using a large piece of paper, begin the session by challenging a member of the group to a game. Draw a grid as used in noughts and crosses but be careful not to call it that. Begin the game as you would a normal game of noughts and crosses but introduce random reasons why the young person you are playing against can't make their moves. These rules could be anything from: 'You can't place an X in a square adjacent to two squares with an O in them', to: 'You can only make your move when standing on one leg.' Add rules randomly as you go through each game, ensuring that they make it impossible for your opponent to win. Once you win again, challenge another young person to a game, once more adding random rules. Eventually one of the young people will point out that it's not fair. Ask the group:

● Why can't any of you win? (Because the rules keep changing.)
● Why are the rules important? (They mean that everyone knows how to play the game.)

Laws of the Game

(15 minutes)

Divide the young people into smaller groups and give each group a piece of paper and a marker. Tell them to imagine that they are explaining the rules of football to someone who has never played the game or seen it played. Get each group to write down as many of the rules of football as they can think of – they could include simple, as well as more complicated, rules of the game.

Resource sheet 4a provides a summary of some of the basic rules of the game.
For a more comprehensive explanation of the rules of football, go to FIFA's web site:
www.fifa.com/documents/fifa/laws/LOTG2005_e.pdf.

Once each group has come up with their list of rules, get them to join with the other groups and compare rules. Ask the young people to think about the following questions:

● Which rule (or rules) is the most important?
● Which rule (or rules) do they think could be scrapped?
● What would happen in a football game if there were no rules?
● Why do we need rules? (We need rules in order for things to work properly – if a football team is going to win a game, they need to know the rules, and stick to them, otherwise they'll get disqualified.)

The big ten

(10 minutes)

Ask the group if they can think of any rules that God has given his people. Explain that after God had rescued his people from Egypt, he gave them some rules to follow – rules we now know as the Ten Commandments. They were there to give the Israelites some boundaries. They were guidelines for how they were supposed to live in the Promised Land.

Get the group to come up with as many of the Commandments as they can remember and then look up the Ten Commandments in Exodus 20. As they read them through, make sure that they understand what each Commandment means. Below are some suggestions for how you might simplify them to make them easier to understand:

1   Don't worship any other God.
2   Don't have idols.
3   Don't misuse God's name.

4 Have one day a week when you spend time resting.
5 Respect people who look after you, like your mum and dad.
6 Don't kill.
7 Be faithful to your husband or wife.
8 Don't steal.
9 Don't lie.
10 Don't want things that aren't yours.

Get the group to think about the following questions:
- Are there any Commandments that they think are particularly hard to keep to?
- Are there any that they think are no longer relevant?

Help me when it's hard

(*5 minutes*)

All of us find it hard to stick to all the rules all the time, but sometimes there are one or two rules that we find that bit harder to keep than the others. Hand out a card to each person and encourage them to think about which of the Ten Commandments (or perhaps other rules they have in their lives) they find it particularly hard to stick to.

Have a time of quiet and ask each member of the group to write a prayer on their card asking God to help them not to break the rules they find hard. Finish with a prayer, either your own or the one below.

Dear God,
Thank you that you love us enough to give us rules
    to help us know how to live our lives.
Help us to try to obey these rules,
    even when they seem unfair or difficult.
Amen.

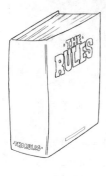

Laws of the Game

Below is a short summary of some of the very basic rules of the game of football.

- The game should be played on a rectangular pitch, between 90 and 120 m long and between 45 m and 90 m wide. The pitch will be marked out with white lines no wider than 12 cm.

- The goalposts should be 7.32 m apart, and the crossbar should be 2.44 m off the ground. They should be white.

- The game is played with a spherical ball measuring not more than 70 cm all the way round and weighing not more than 450 g.

- A match is played by two teams, each of which consists of eleven players, including one goalkeeper.

- Each player has to wear a football shirt, shorts, socks, shin-pads and football boots. The goalkeeper should wear a different coloured top from everyone else.

- Each game should have a referee whose job it is to observe and enforce the rules, monitor the timings and ensure the safety of all the players.

- The teams play for a total of 90 minutes. Halfway through the game, players are entitled to a break of not more than 15 minutes. Time lost (for example, because of injury) is added on to the second half.

- The game begins with a kick-off from the centre line.

- A goal is scored when the whole of the ball passes over the goal line, between the goalposts and under the crossbar, provided that no other rules are broken in the process.

- The team that scores the greater number of goals by the end of the match is declared the winner. If both teams score the same number of goals, or if no goals are scored, then the match is declared to be a draw.

- A player is declared offside and a free kick is awarded to the other team if they are nearer to the opposition's goal line than both the ball and the second last opponent, unless the player receives the ball directly from a goal kick, throw-in or a corner, or they are in their own half of the pitch, or they are level with the second last or last two opponents.

For more detailed rules, have a look at the FIFA Laws of the Game, which can be found on their web site at: www.fifa.com/documents/fifa/laws/LOTG2005_e.pdf.

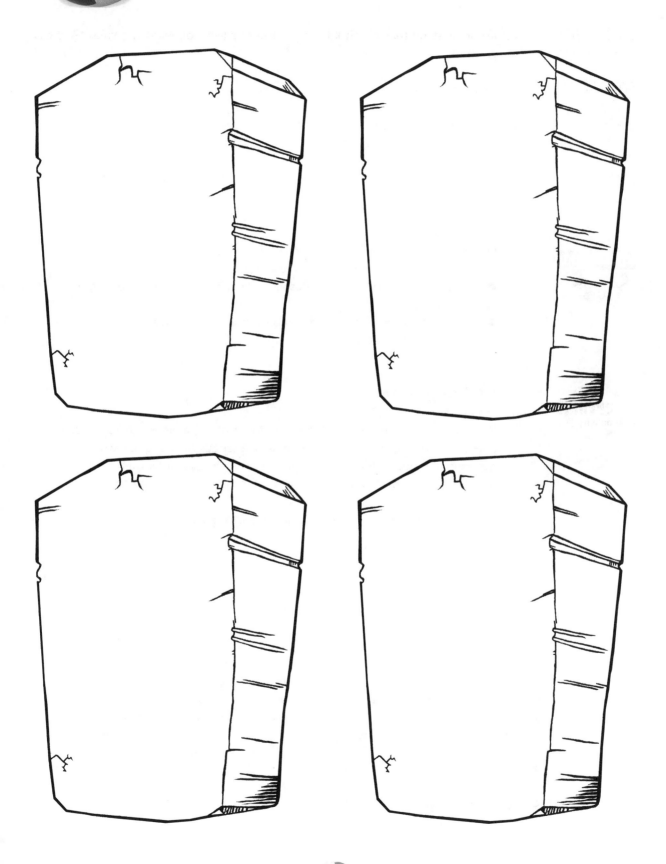

Red Card

LIVING LIFE ACCORDING TO GOD'S RULES

SESSION AIM........ **To understand that we should try to live our lives following the rules God has given us**

FOOTBALL FOCUS.... Red and yellow cards

BIBLE FOCUS....... 'Similarly, if anyone competes as an athlete, he does not receive the victor's crown unless he competes according to the rules.' (2 Timothy 2.5)

RESOURCES......... *Copies of Resource sheet 5a for the first activity, red and yellow card, Bible, pens, copies of Resource sheet 5b*

BEFOREHAND

- Photocopy on to white card and cut up the rules on Resource sheet 5a: enough copies to give one set to each group.
- Photocopy enough copies of Resource sheet 5b to give one to each pair of young people.
- Cut up the yellow and red card into cards about the size of a postcard, one for each young person.

OPENING activity

Red or yellow

(15 minutes)

Remind the young people that during a football match, if a player breaks a rule, the referee will hand him a red card (for breaking a serious rule) or a yellow card (not quite such a serious rule). A player who is given a red card or two yellow cards will be sent off the field and not allowed to play for the rest of the match.

Divide the young people into groups, and give each group a set of the photocopied cards (Resource sheet 5a). Give the groups 10 minutes to decide which of the offences mean that a player gets given a yellow card, and which result in a red card. Once they have put the cards into two sets, go through the answers using the list below.

Yellow cards can be awarded for	*Red cards can be awarded for*
<ul><li>Unsporting behaviour</li><li>Disagreeing with the referee</li><li>Persistently breaking the rules</li><li>Delaying the restart of play</li><li>Defenders not staying the proper distance away from the kicker on a corner or free kick</li><li>Entering the field without the referee's permission</li><li>Deliberately leaving the field without the referee's permission.</li></ul>	<ul><li>Serious foul</li><li>Violent conduct</li><li>Spitting at anyone</li><li>A deliberate 'hand ball' to deny an obvious goal-scoring opportunity</li><li>Fouling an opponent to prevent an obvious goal-scoring opportunity</li><li>Using offensive or threatening language</li><li>Receiving a second yellow card during a game.</li></ul>

If you have more space (for instance, if you are meeting in a hall), you can make the activity more physical. Place the cards at one end of the hall, position the teams in the middle, and then place two chairs for each team (one for red card offences and one for yellow card offences) at the other end of the hall. When the game starts, a team member has to run to collect a card and bring it back to the team. The team decide if it's a red or yellow card offence and then a team member runs and puts it on to the appropriate chair. Each team can only move one card at a time. The game ends as soon as one of the teams has worked through all their cards. Go through the answers using the list above. The winning team is the first team to sort out all the cards correctly.

Rules are made to be …
(15 minutes)
Divide the young people into pairs and give each pair a copy of Resource sheet 5b. Get each pair to begin by writing down what the punishments are for breaking each of the rules on the sheet. Once they've done that, in the blank boxes at the foot of the sheet, get them to write some of their own examples of rules they have to follow – they might be rules within the youth group, rules at school, rules at home or general rules in life.

Once the pairs have filled in as much as of the sheet as they can, get the group to consider the following questions:
● Which punishments do the group think are fair?
● Why do we have punishments for breaking rules?
● Does the group think these punishments are too strict or too lenient?
● What would happen if there were no punishments when someone broke a rule?

Towards the victor's crown
(10 minutes)
Get the group to look up 2 Timothy 2.5, and then consider the following questions:
● What was Paul trying to say to Timothy about how God wants us to live our lives? (God wants us to try to live according to the rules he has given us.)
● Which rules do you think Paul was referring to? (The commandments Jesus gave his followers, based on the Ten Commandments given to Moses; Paul was also referring to the rules of the land in which we live.)
● What happens when we don't obey rules? (It makes things a lot harder for us, and we don't do as well as God wants us to. **Note**: it does *not* mean that if we don't keep to the rules, we won't get to heaven!
● Do there have to be punishments for not keeping to the rules? Why?

Card carrying
(10 minutes)
Hand out the red and yellow cards to members of the group. Explain that we all find some rules much harder to keep – sometimes we fail and break rules we know we shouldn't. Get the young people to spend a few moments thinking about rules they find it hard to keep. It might be a rule the Bible talks about or one that's been set by parents or teachers. Get them to write a prayer on their card asking God to help them to keep to that rule.

Once everyone has written their prayer, finish the session with a prayer – use a prayer of your own or the one below.

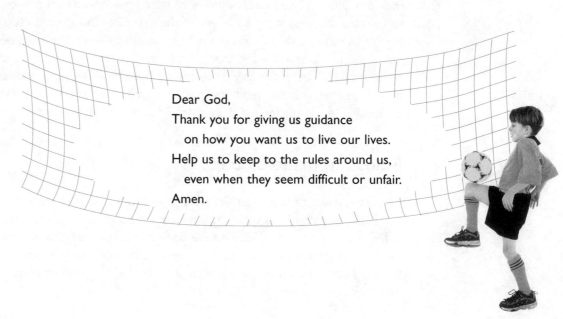

Dear God,
Thank you for giving us guidance
    on how you want us to live our lives.
Help us to keep to the rules around us,
    even when they seem difficult or unfair.
Amen.

Unsporting behaviour	Fouling an opponent to stop someone scoring a goal
Spitting at anyone	Violent conduct
Delaying the restart of play	Serious foul play
Disagreeing with the referee	A deliberate hand ball to stop someone scoring a goal
Persistently breaking the rules	Using offensive or threatening language
Receiving a second yellow card during a game	Entering the field without the referee's permission
Defenders not staying the proper distance away from the kicker on a corner or free kick	Deliberately leaving the field without the referee's permission

THE PUNISHMENT FITS THE CRIME?!?!

BREAKING A SCHOOL WINDOW →

KILLING SOMEONE →

STEALING SWEETS FROM A SHOP →

NOT HANDING IN YOUR HOMEWORK →

→

→

League tables
BEING FIRST

SESSION AIM . . . . . . **To understand that being 'top' or 'best' or 'first' is not a priority for God**

FOOTBALL FOCUS . . . League tables

BIBLE FOCUS . . . . . . 'A man was there by the name of Zacchaeus; he was a chief tax collector and was wealthy. He wanted to see who Jesus was, but being a short man he could not, because of the crowd. So he ran ahead and climbed a sycamore-fig tree to see him, since Jesus was coming that way. When Jesus reached the spot, he looked up and said to him, "Zacchaeus, come down immediately. I must stay at your house today." So he came down at once and welcomed him gladly. All the people saw this and began to mutter, "He has gone to be the guest of a 'sinner'." But Zacchaeus stood up and said to the Lord, "Look, Lord! Here and now I give half of my possessions to the poor, and if I have cheated anybody out of anything, I will pay back four times the amount." Jesus said to him, "Today salvation has come to this house, because this man, too, is a son of Abraham. For the Son of Man came to seek and to save what was lost."' (Luke 19.2-10)

RESOURCES . . . . *Football, list of teams in different leagues, Bible, pens, paper, wooden spoon*

- Look up who is currently in the Premiership. (If you are doing this session outside the football season, find out how the table looked at the end of the last season.) The BBC Football web site is a good source for this kind of information. It can be accessed at: http://news.bbc.co.uk/sport1/hi/football/default.stm.

League tables
(5 minutes)

To begin this session, get the group to stand in a circle. Tell them that you are going to throw the football to a member of the group and as they catch the ball they have to name a team in the Premiership (the top division in the Football League). They then throw the ball to someone else in the circle. If they drop the ball or can't think of a team, they are out and have to sit down. You could then play the same game with the championship or the league in which your local teams play.

Ask the group why they think we have league tables for football teams – what's the point?

Number 1 at . . .
(15 minutes)

Explain that we are going to come up with some league tables within the group. Devise some simple tasks that test particular skills within the group. You might see who can do the most star jumps (if you have a more active group) or who can name the most Simpsons characters.

After testing the group on each skill, create a league table for that skill – make sure you include a variety of tasks so that group members appear in different orders on each table. Once you've finished your league tables, discuss the following questions:

- How does it feel to be at the top of the table?
- How does it feel to be at the bottom of the league?
- Why is it better to be at the top rather than the bottom – what are the advantages?

FOCUS
on Bible passage

Good ol' Zach

(*10 minutes*)

The Bible is full of instances of people ignoring league tables! Jesus was especially good at this. He chose people from the bottom of the league to be his friends and companions, and he told stories about people who weren't climbing up the table!

As a good example, get the group to look up the story of Zacchaeus in Luke chapter 19. Ask:

- How important and successful was Zacchaeus – was he at the top or bottom of the table? (As a tax collector, he would have been quite rich and would have occupied a position of authority within the community.)
- Where would he have been on the popularity league table? (Very low down, if not bottom – he cheated people out of their money and worked for the enemy.)
- Why did Jesus choose to visit Zacchaeus' house? (Jesus didn't care how important or successful or hated Zacchaeus was – he just saw someone who needed to change his ways.)

PRAYER
response

'The last shall be . . .'

(*10 minutes*)

Get the group to think about people they know who are always bottom of the league – they might think about people who aren't very good at sport or who others think aren't very clever or who always have the wrong clothes.

Sit the group in a circle and pass round the wooden spoon (often given to teams in last place as a 'booby prize'). As each person takes the spoon, get them to pray for one of the people they've thought of, asking God to be with that person. Finish with a short prayer, either of your own choosing or the one below.

Dear God,
Help us to remember that being first isn't everything.
Thank you that you don't care whether we are top or bottom.
Help us look out for those people
    who never seem to be at the top.
Amen.

Salaries
MONEY

SESSION AIM....... **To think about our attitude to money**

FOOTBALL FOCUS... Football players' salaries

BIBLE FOCUS....... 'Do not store up for yourselves treasures on earth, where moth and rust destroy, and where thieves break in and steal. But store up for yourselves treasures in heaven, where moth and rust do not destroy, and where thieves do not break in and steal. For where your treasure is, there your heart will be also.' (Matthew 6.19-21)

RESOURCES......... *1p coins, pens, pieces of paper, box or container, Bible*

- Find enough 1p coins to give one to each member of the group.

Who wants to be a millionaire?
(*10 minutes*)
Begin the session by handing everyone a piece of paper and a pen. Get the young people to imagine that they have each just been given £1 million. What could they buy with that much money? Start by discussing their ideas in general: you might find that they have only a hazy concept of how large a sum £1 million is!

Once the young people have some understanding of what £1 million could buy, get each member of the group to write down, without telling anyone, how they would spend the money. Tell them to fold their papers in half without signing them. Collect them in and put them in a container. Then draw them out one by one. Can the group guess whose is whose?

Super salaries
(*10 minutes*)
We'd all like more money than we have, and we can all think of lots of exciting things we'd do with it if we had it. Footballers are known to be paid an awful lot, but how much do people in different football-related professions get paid?

Give each person a piece of paper and a pen. Start by naming a profession, using the list below, and then get the young people to write down how much they think that person might earn. Once everyone has written their answer, get them to reveal their guesses. Tell them who was closest to the correct amount. Keep going until you have guessed the salaries of all six professions. Below are the average salaries for six football-related professions. (These figures were correct at the end of 2006. You may wish to find more recent figures.)

- PE Teacher – £19,000 per year
- Sports journalist – £30,000 per year
- Professional Premiership referee – £50,000 per year
- Manager of the National Football Museum – £35,000 per year
- Coach for England's football squad – £4,500,000 per year
- English Premiership footballer (average salary in 2006) – £676,000 per year

FOCUS
on Bible passage

Money! Money! Money!

(10 minutes)

We talk a lot about money – how much people earn, how much things cost and how much money people have are all questions that regularly make it to the front pages of our newspapers. Yet often the people who have lots of money aren't the people who are happy with life – they seem to have everything, yet have not found happiness through what they have.

The Bible shows us a different set of priorities. Get the group to look up Matthew 6.19-21 and think about the following questions:
- Why do these verses say that we shouldn't focus on having lots of money? (Because while it might seem great at the time, it won't last for ever!)
- What do these verses say we should focus on instead of money? (We should focus on what God thinks is important.)
- How can we store up riches in heaven? (By doing the things God wants us to do and living our lives as he commanded.)
- What do these words in verse 21 mean: 'For where your treasure is, there your heart will be also'?(One possible paraphrase might be that people care most about the things they focus their lives on.)

PRAYER
response

Penny prayers

(10 minutes)

Give a 1p coin to each member of the group and explain that having thought about money, we're going to use these coins to help us pray. Use each of the aspects of a 1p coin listed below as the topic for a prayer. After introducing each topic, either pause for silent reflection, or get the young people to add their own prayers on that theme. The different aspects of the 1p are:
- The portcullis (pray for those imprisoned)
- The Queen's head (pray for those who lead our country)
- The round shape (pray for the world)
- The number 1 (pray for unity)
- The date (pray for today and the coming week).

Finish with a prayer of your own or use the prayer below.

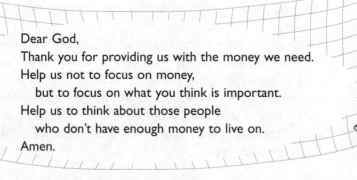

Dear God,
Thank you for providing us with the money we need.
Help us not to focus on money,
    but to focus on what you think is important.
Help us to think about those people
    who don't have enough money to live on.
Amen.

Team tactics
THE CHURCH AS A BODY

SESSION AIM....... **To think about people in the church working as different parts of a team**

FOOTBALL FOCUS.... The different roles that people play in a football team

BIBLE FOCUS....... 'The body is a unit, though it is made up of many parts; and though all its parts are many, they form one body. So it is with Christ. For we were all baptized by one Spirit into one body —whether Jews or Greeks, slave or free — and we were all given the one Spirit to drink. Now the body is not made up of one part but of many. If the foot should say, "Because I am not a hand, I do not belong to the body," it would not for that reason cease to be part of the body. And if the ear should say, "Because I am not an eye, I do not belong to the body," it would not for that reason cease to be part of the body. If the whole body were an eye, where would the sense of hearing be? If the whole body were an ear, where would the sense of smell be? But in fact God has arranged the parts in the body, every one of them, just as he wanted them to be. If they were all one part, where would the body be? As it is, there are many parts, but one body. The eye cannot say to the hand, "I don't need you!" And the head cannot say to the feet, "I don't need you!" On the contrary, those parts of the body that seem to be weaker are indispensable, and the parts that we think are less honourable we treat with special honour. And the parts that are unpresentable are treated with special modesty, while our presentable parts need no special treatment. But God has combined the members of the body and has given greater honour to the parts that lacked it, so that there should be no division in the body, but that its parts should have equal concern for each other.' (1 Corinthians 12.12-25)

RESOURCES......... *Football, large sheet of paper, marker, Bible, background music, copies of Resource sheet 8 on card*

BEFOREHAND

● Print out copies of Resource sheet 8 on to card and cut them up ready for use in the prayer activity: enough copies to allow a good choice of body parts.

OPENING activity

Part of the team
(10 minutes)

Begin the session by getting the group to stand in a circle. Tell them that you are going to throw the football to one of them and as they catch the ball they are to name the job of someone involved in helping to run a football team. Get them to be specific, for example, to say 'goalie' rather than 'player', and to think more widely than just the eleven players on the team. Once they have called out a role or position, they throw the ball to another member of the group who calls out a job. Anyone who repeats what has already been said, or can't think of anything, is out and sits down. The game carries on until everyone is out.

While the game is going, keep a running list of the roles that the group come up with. Write these on a large piece of paper.

FOCUS
on football

Top of the pile

(15 minutes)

Once the group has come up with a list of people involved in running a football team, divide the young people into pairs or small groups. In their groups, get them to pick the two most important people on the list, and identify what they do that makes them so important. Then suggest the two that a football team could most easily do without.

Give the small groups time to discuss their choices, and then feed back to the whole group, giving their reasons.

FOCUS
on Bible passage

Heads and hands

(10 minutes)

The Bible talks about the importance of teamwork – and about how the church needs to be like a team. Get the group to read 1 Corinthians 12.12-25 and discuss the following questions:

● Do they agree with what Paul was writing – is every member of a team as important as all the others?
● Has anyone in the group ever wanted to play a different part in the team – why?
● How might you rewrite verses 14 and 15 to refer to a football team rather than a body?
● What would happen if the manager decided to play as a defender and the striker decided to become the football club's accountant? (The football team wouldn't work as well!)
● What jobs do people do as part of the church?
● Which job in a church do the group think is the most important? Why?

We all have different roles and jobs as part of a group of Christians and all the jobs are equally important, no matter what we might think.

PRAYER
response

Body bits

(10 minutes)

Lay the pictures of the different body parts (copied from Resource sheet 8) on the floor in the middle of the group. Play some quiet music, and get the members of the group to think about what they might be good at – what talents and skills do they have that could be used within the body of the church? Are they good at listening to other people, or at making things with their hands, or at talking to others, or at being kind to others? Or are they good at something else? Once they've thought of something, encourage them to pick up a picture of the body part that represents that talent and write a short prayer on it asking God to help them to use their talent to help the Body of Christ.

When everyone has written their prayer, finish with a short prayer of your own choosing or use the one below.

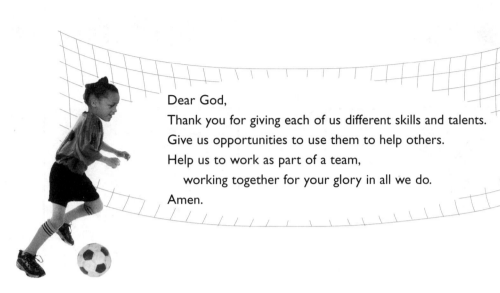

Dear God,
Thank you for giving each of us different skills and talents.
Give us opportunities to use them to help others.
Help us to work as part of a team,
    working together for your glory in all we do.
Amen.

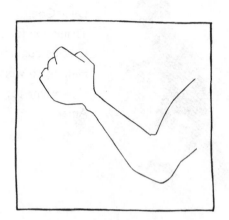
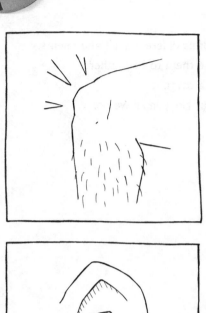
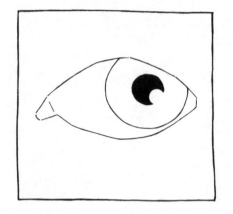
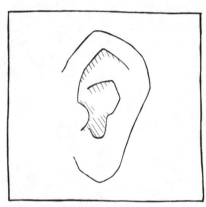
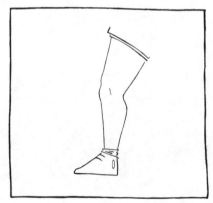
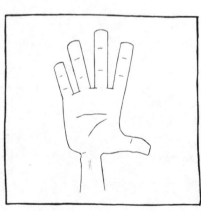
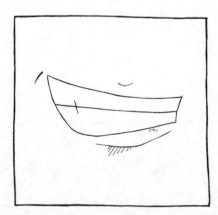
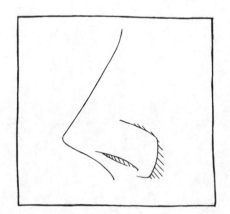

Here we go! Here we go! Here we go! WORSHIP

9

SESSION AIM....... **To think about why Christians worship God with songs**

FOCUS........... Football chants

BIBLE FOCUS....... 'It is good to praise the LORD
and make music to your name, O Most High,
to proclaim your love in the morning
and your faithfulness at night,
to the music of the ten-stringed lyre
and the melody of the harp.
For you make me glad by your deeds, O LORD;
I sing for joy at the works of your hands.
How great are your works, O LORD,
how profound your thoughts!' (Psalm 92.1-5)

RESOURCES......... *Sweets as prizes, Bible, paper, pens, background music, copies of Resource sheet 9*

- Find out about any local football chants.
- Photocopy enough copies of Resource sheet 9 to give one to each person.

Name that tune
(*10 minutes*)
Begin the session by asking the group to complete the following football chants and identify the club that has adopted each one:
- 'One nil to the . . .' (Arsenal)
- 'Glory glory . . .' (Manchester United)
- 'You'll never walk alone' (Liverpool)
- 'Blue is the colour' (Chelsea)
- 'I'm forever blowing bubbles' (West Ham)

Ask the group if any of them know any other football chants, ensuring that they realize you only want to hear clean ones!

Either in small groups, or all together, get the young people to think about why fans have football chants. It might help to think about the topics of the chants and when the chants are used.

Write the ideas that the young people come up with on a large piece of paper so you can refer back to them later. Some possible ideas could include:
- encouraging the team/players;
- making the fans feel part of a group;
- celebrating a goal or victory.

Worship chants

(10 minutes)

Explain to the group that although chants at football matches and hymns in church obviously focus on very different subjects, and use very different words, there are similarities between the reasons why people shout football chants and why they sing songs and choruses to praise God. Get the group to name any songs that they know are sung in churches, or during school assemblies – give out prizes to anyone who is prepared to sing a few lines from one!

Read the following quotation from a book by Marcus Green in which he says that worshipping God is like chanting a football chant:

> **Worship is like the great cheer echoing around a football stadium as the critical goal is scored. Like the roar of the crowd, worship tells us that something has happened which has made a difference to the way things are. And as we listen to the chant, we can tell who scored the goal.**
>
> (Marcus Green, *Salvation's Song*, Kingsway, 2004)

- Why do the group think Marcus Green thought that worshipping God was a bit like singing a football chant at a football match? (People want to celebrate the amazing things God has done with the same enthusiasm and excitement that football fans have at a football match.)

Praise God!

(10 minutes)

Introduce the book of Psalms to the group, explaining that some chants written by King David that tell God how great he is can be found here in this Old Testament book of the Bible. Get the group to look up Psalm 92.1-5.

- When does the psalmist (the person who wrote the psalm) say we should praise God? (In the morning and the night – the psalmist means we should praise God all the time.)
- Why does the psalmist say we should praise God? (Because of the great things God has done for us.)

Refer back to the list of reasons why people chant at football matches and ask:

- How many of these reasons could apply to why Christians sing songs to worship God?

Christians feel as passionate about God and what he has done as football fans feel about their teams, and one of the ways they show this is through songs and chants of worship. It is worth pointing out that songs and chants are not the only way in which we can worship God – they are just one out of many ways.

Own song

(10 minutes)

Give each young person a copy of Resource sheet 9 and put out some pens. Explain that there will be a short period of quiet while they think up their own psalm or chant. It can be as long or as short, as simple or as complex, as they like, and should focus on how they feel about God. Both football chants and songs of worship to God often focus on how the person feels. Reassure the young people that they are not going to have to share what they write – it's a chance for them to write something that tells God how they feel. Play some music as they write.

Finish with a short prayer, either of your own choosing or the one below.

Dear God,

Thank you for the wonderful things you have done for us.

Help us to praise you, as David did.

Help us to remember to worship you both in song
and also in the way we live our lives.

Amen.

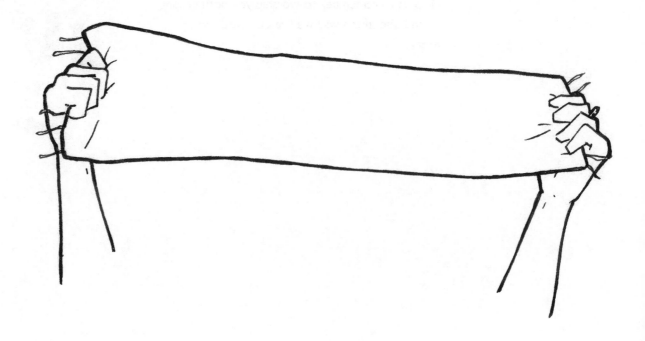

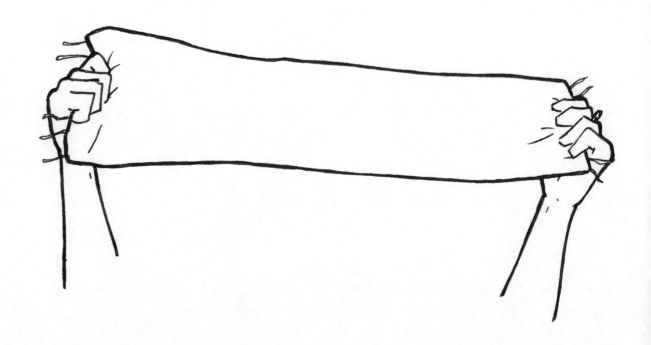

Equipment
THE ARMOUR OF GOD

SESSION AIM....... **To think about what equipment we have to help us live as Christians**

FOOTBALL FOCUS.... Equipment needed to play football

BIBLE FOCUS....... 'Therefore put on the full armour of God, so that when the day of evil comes, you may be able to stand your ground, and after you have done everything, to stand. Stand firm then, with the belt of truth buckled around your waist, with the breastplate of righteousness in place, and with your feet fitted with the readiness that comes from the gospel of peace. In addition to all this, take up the shield of faith, with which you can extinguish all the flaming arrows of the evil one. Take the helmet of salvation and the sword of the Spirit, which is the word of God.' (Ephesians 6.13-17)

RESOURCES......... *Paper, pens, newspapers, Sellotape, markers, scissors, prize, plastic cutlery*

- A clipboard and a sheet of paper giving the list of football equipment (see the first activity).

Can you guess what it is yet?
(5 minutes)
Divide the young people into groups. Get a representative from each group to come up and get the name of a piece of football equipment. They have to go back to their group and mime this piece of equipment, without saying anything or making any noise at all. Once a member of the group guesses the answer correctly, they come up and get the name of the next piece of equipment. The winning team is the first team to guess all the words.
- Football
- Shin-pad
- Goalpost
- Referee's whistle
- Linesman's flag
- Football stud
- Captain's armband
- Clipboard
- Football pump

Ready to go?
(15 minutes)
Whether we're playing football or baking a cake, we need the right equipment to help us get the job done properly.

Divide the young people into small groups. Tell them that you have a list of everyday tasks. When you call out the first task, their group has 30 seconds to write down all the pieces of equipment that they would need to carry out that task. Say that after 30 seconds, you will ask one person from each group to call out the items on their list. Each group will get one point for every piece of equipment they have (that would actually be used!) that no other group has thought of. Work through the list, each time seeing which group has won. Examples of tasks might include baking a cake, washing the car, having a bath, doing your homework. The last task you give the group should be 'living like a Christian'.

Once you've worked out the overall winning group, look back at the list of equipment the groups came up with for helping people to live like a Christian. Talk through the lists, exploring the different ideas. Then ask:
● When might Christians need this equipment? (There are always going to be times when we need help living our lives the way God wants us to – we need certain equipment, skills and characteristics to help us along the way.)

on Bible passage

Full body armour
(15 minutes)
Explain that the Bible talks about the equipment God gives us to help us live like Christians, and refers to it as 'the armour of God'. Divide the young people into small groups and give each group some newspaper, some Sellotape and a Bible. Each group has 10 minutes to construct the armour Paul talks about, using a member of the group as a model and the description of the armour given by Paul in Ephesians 6.13-17. Award a prize for the most armour-like creation!

response

Tools for the job
(10 minutes)
Each of us needs help to live our lives as God wants. God gives us tools and we all need to learn to use them more effectively. Give each member of the group a piece of plastic cutlery and explain that this represents the tools we've been given.

Get the young people to think about the list in the Ephesians passage and decide which tools they would like to become more skilled at using. Write these down on the cutlery.

Finish with a short prayer asking for God's help. Either use a prayer of your own or the prayer below.

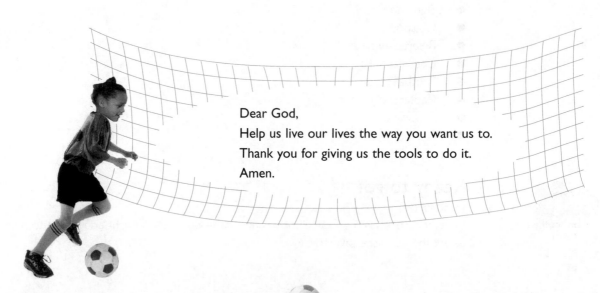

Dear God,
Help us live our lives the way you want us to.
Thank you for giving us the tools to do it.
Amen.